AI Video Marketing

Create Viral Shorts, Reels, and Ads With Zero Editing Skills

By Joe Correa

Published by Live Stronger Faster

This book is for educational and informational purposes only. The author and publisher are not engaged in rendering legal, financial, or other professional advice. Readers should consult a qualified professional before making any financial decisions.

First Edition

Table of Contents

Introduction 5

Chapter 1: The New Era of AI Video Creation 10

Chapter 2: From Script to Screen — How to Turn Ideas Into Viral Videos With AI 17

Chapter 3: Mastering Faceless Video Marketing 24

Chapter 4: AI Storytelling Secrets — How to Hook, Engage, and Retain Viewers in 30 Seconds 31

Chapter 5: AI Video Ads That Convert — How to Sell Without Sounding Salesy 38

Chapter 6: Automating Video Production — How to Build a 24/7 Content Machine With AI 45

Chapter 7: Monetizing AI Video Content — From Views to Income Streams 52

Chapter 8: AI Video Analytics — Tracking Performance, Growth, and ROI 59

Chapter 9: Scaling Your AI Video Brand — Building a Global Audience With Automation 67

Chapter 10: The Future of AI Video Marketing — Evolving With the Next Wave of Innovation 75

Epilogue 82

Introduction

In today's digital landscape, attention has become the most valuable currency. You can have the best product, the most compelling story, or the most generous offer — but if no one stops to watch your video, none of it matters. What separates creators who explode online from those who struggle for views is not just creativity; it's speed, precision, and timing. The rise of short-form video platforms like YouTube Shorts, Instagram Reels, and TikTok has completely changed the marketing game. And now, Artificial Intelligence has changed it again. With tools like InVideo, OpusClip, Pictory, and Synthesia, you can go from idea to viral video in minutes — without recording yourself, without editing software, and without expensive equipment. This book will show you exactly how.

AI video marketing is more than just automation — it's creative amplification. It allows anyone, regardless of skill level, to create cinematic-quality videos that engage, convert, and scale. Think about what used to take professional editors hours: trimming footage, adding subtitles, optimizing formats for each platform, creating thumbnails, and matching background music. AI now performs all of that automatically — while learning from millions of data points to predict what works best for each audience. The result is a world where storytelling meets science. You no longer have to be a filmmaker to capture attention. You just need the right AI workflow.

In this book, you'll discover how to use AI to produce viral content consistently. You'll learn how to research trending topics using AI tools, generate scripts in seconds, and turn those scripts into professional faceless videos that build your brand 24/7. You'll see how creators and entrepreneurs are using AI-powered video systems to grow their audiences to millions, build loyal communities, and generate recurring income. From micro-influencers to large brands, the competitive advantage today belongs to those who can move fast – and AI video tools make that speed possible. Whether you're an entrepreneur, educator, real estate professional, coach, or small business owner, this book will help you replace time-consuming manual video production with smart AI automation that multiplies your output and profits.

The foundation of this transformation lies in the convergence of three forces: automation, personalization, and accessibility. First, AI automates every step of video creation – from scriptwriting to editing, subtitles, and social posting. Second, it personalizes every output to the platform and audience. You can tell an AI video generator to create ten different versions of the same video, each adapted for YouTube, Instagram, TikTok, and Facebook. The captions, timing, aspect ratios, and even emotional tones can all change automatically. Third, accessibility has reached an all-time high. With simple drag-and-drop interfaces, anyone can produce professional videos using a browser or smartphone. AI video marketing is not reserved for tech experts — it's designed for everyday creators who want to share their message, grow their brand, and get paid doing it.

Imagine this: You upload one long video, maybe a product demo or a podcast interview, and within minutes AI automatically cuts it into dozens of high-performing short clips optimized for every platform. The AI identifies emotional peaks, audience retention triggers, and hooks — the exact moments that would go viral — and then adds captions, emojis, and titles. This is what tools like OpusClip do with astonishing accuracy. Combined with InVideo for fast script-to-video generation, Pictory for automated video summarization, and Synthesia for human-like AI avatars, you now have the ultimate content studio in your browser. You can create talking-head style explainer videos with AI presenters who speak in your brand voice, or generate faceless video reels that inspire, educate, and sell while you sleep. The barrier to entry has vanished. The only limitation is how quickly you can implement what you're about to learn.

But mastering AI video marketing isn't just about pressing buttons — it's about strategy. This book will teach you how to combine creativity with data. You'll learn how to identify viral trends before they peak using AI-driven analytics, craft the perfect hook and structure your videos for retention, and use AI editing techniques to maintain energy and flow. You'll also learn how to automate your posting schedule, track performance with AI analytics, and even A/B test different video variations to find the top performer. Every chapter in this book builds a complete system — from ideation to execution — designed to generate consistent visibility, leads, and income. The goal is not just to make more videos, but to make smarter videos that convert.

As we move further into the AI era, video content is no longer optional — it's the foundation of digital success. Studies show that 82% of all online traffic is video. Algorithms favor it, audiences prefer it, and conversion rates skyrocket when video is involved. Yet, only a small percentage of creators and businesses truly leverage it because of one reason: production complexity. That's the exact problem AI solves. You don't need to hire editors, videographers, or voice actors. AI handles every step. You can even clone your voice, choose from hundreds of AI-generated narrators, or let the system select visuals and music that match your message automatically. The playing field has been leveled. The next wave of top creators will be those who understand how to integrate AI into every stage of content creation.

By the time you finish this book, you'll have the power to create entire campaigns in hours instead of weeks. You'll be able to build faceless YouTube channels, generate viral Instagram reels, and produce high-converting video ads — all without touching a camera. You'll also learn how to systemize your content so it keeps working for you long after it's published. This is not about chasing trends — it's about building a lasting digital presence powered by AI. Each chapter will walk you through the exact tools, workflows, and monetization strategies used by top creators who are quietly earning six and seven figures a year using AI video marketing systems.

You're about to enter a world where marketing is faster, smarter, and more human than ever — even when it's created by machines. AI doesn't remove the human element; it enhances it. It gives you more time to think, create, and connect. It allows you to focus on storytelling while AI handles the technical work. The new era of marketing belongs to those who can merge creativity with automation — those who can build emotional connections at scale through video, without sacrificing authenticity. This book is your blueprint to make that possible.

Welcome to the **AI Video Marketing Revolution** – where you can create viral shorts, reels, and ads with zero editing skills, unlimited potential, and full creative control. Let's begin.

Chapter 1: The New Era of AI Video Creation

The video marketing world has entered a turning point so massive that it's rewriting the rules of content creation, advertising, and brand storytelling all at once. For decades, success in video required expensive cameras, complex software, and technical know-how. The early days of YouTube and Facebook rewarded only those who could afford production crews or editing skills. But today, Artificial Intelligence has flipped that hierarchy upside down. The same level of quality that once took a studio and a team can now be achieved by a single person with a laptop and an AI video generator. This is the new era of video creation — one where time, budget, and talent are no longer barriers, and where creative ideas matter more than production limitations.

AI video tools such as **InVideo**, **OpusClip**, **Pictory**, and **Synthesia** are not just productivity hacks; they represent the democratization of media. Anyone with a message, a product, or a story can now turn it into professional content within minutes. You can paste a script or even a rough outline into an AI platform and receive a finished video complete with narration, stock footage, captions, transitions, and music. You can select a tone — inspiring, educational, cinematic, humorous — and the system will adapt automatically. These tools are built on machine learning models trained on millions of viral videos, which means they recognize the patterns of retention, emotional flow, and engagement that make a viewer stop scrolling and start watching. In essence, you're working with the distilled intelligence of the most successful content ever created.

But the real power of AI video marketing goes beyond automation — it's in **scaling creativity**. Imagine being able to test ten different versions of the same message in one afternoon, each optimized for a different audience or platform. One version could target professionals on LinkedIn with a calm, polished tone, while another grabs TikTok viewers with bold captions and quick cuts. AI handles this multi-platform transformation automatically, ensuring that your message fits the unique culture and algorithmic preferences of each platform. What used to require multiple editors and weeks of coordination now takes minutes. As a marketer or entrepreneur, this gives you something priceless: the ability to out-create and out-test everyone else.

To thrive in this new era, however, you must learn to think like an AI-powered storyteller. It starts with the **idea-to-execution workflow**. Step one is clarity: decide what emotion or outcome you want your audience to feel. Step two is scripting — not long essays, but concise, conversational hooks that AI can easily visualize. Step three is generation: feed that script into tools like InVideo or Synthesia and select your format (horizontal for YouTube, vertical for Shorts or Reels). Step four is optimization: use OpusClip or Pictory to repurpose longer videos into short, high-retention clips. Finally, step five is automation: schedule, publish, and analyze results using AI-powered schedulers that automatically refine future outputs based on engagement data. Once this workflow is set up, your content machine runs on autopilot — learning, adapting, and improving over time.

The business implications are enormous. Coaches are building entire course funnels using only AI-generated video lessons. Real estate agents are creating neighborhood tours using voice-over avatars. E-commerce brands are producing hundreds of short ads a week — each one auto-tested for clicks and conversions. Even large corporations are replacing traditional ad agencies with in-house AI studios that can generate videos faster, cheaper, and more effectively. The line between creator and brand has blurred. Every entrepreneur is now a media company, and AI is the engine powering that transformation.

Still, the key is to **retain authenticity**. The most successful AI creators are not the ones who hide behind automation but the ones who use it to amplify their personality and message. Your tone, your storytelling rhythm, your visual choices — these become your signature. Use AI to free your time, not replace your voice. The viewers of tomorrow will be drawn to creators who blend intelligence and emotion, precision and passion. AI gives you the canvas; your humanity provides the art.

This book will help you master that balance. You'll learn the best prompts for script generation, the ideal video structures for retention, and the editing tricks that trigger watch-time growth. You'll explore faceless video strategies that work even if you're camera-shy, and you'll understand how to build an automated posting system that keeps your channels growing while you focus on strategy. By the end of this chapter, you'll see why AI video marketing is not a passing trend — it's a permanent evolution in how ideas spread, audiences grow, and brands are built.

The truth is simple: in this new era, attention is algorithmic. Success doesn't depend on who has the biggest camera, but who can create the most content that resonates, fast. AI allows you to compress months of production into minutes and to compete with the biggest brands on equal ground. The revolution isn't coming — it's already here. The only question is whether you'll adapt fast enough to lead it.

"The Creator Who Filmed Without a Camera"

When Mia Alvarez lost her marketing job, she didn't own a camera, a microphone, or a lighting setup. All she had was a laptop, a dream, and a burning question: how do I start over when I have nothing left to sell but my ideas? She'd always loved teaching small business owners how to attract customers online, but creating videos had always felt impossible. She had tried editing before — hours spent trimming clips, syncing audio, and choosing stock footage. The process drained her creativity faster than her ambition could recover. But in late 2024, she stumbled upon a YouTube video titled *"How to Create Faceless Reels Using AI."* That single click changed everything.

Within minutes, Mia discovered a universe of tools she'd never imagined. She opened **InVideo**, typed "How to grow your small business online in 60 seconds," and watched in disbelief as the platform generated a complete video: narration, visuals, music — everything. It looked professional, even cinematic. Next, she uploaded an old podcast episode into **OpusClip**, and the AI automatically selected the most engaging 15-second moments, added captions, and suggested hashtags. For the first time, Mia didn't feel behind the camera — she felt ahead of it. The technology wasn't replacing her creativity; it was finally unleashing it. She decided to commit fully. Every morning, she wrote a short motivational script using ChatGPT, uploaded it to InVideo, and turned it into a faceless reel. Every afternoon, she repurposed her older content using OpusClip and **Pictory**, producing 20 to 30 shorts per week. By the end of her first month, one of her AI-generated videos hit 1.2 million views on Instagram. Her follower count exploded, but more importantly, her consulting inquiries tripled. She began receiving messages from people across the world: "How did you make this?" "Can you teach me?" "Do you sell templates?" She realized she had stumbled into something bigger — a system that could create influence and income simultaneously.

Soon, Mia launched her own mini-course titled *"Video Creation for Non-Techies"* — entirely built with AI. Every module was narrated by an AI avatar that resembled her, speaking in her cloned voice from **Synthesia**. She didn't have to record or edit anything. Within 90 days, her course generated $12,000 in sales. What once took her weeks of production now took a few hours of prompting and scheduling. But beyond the income, something deeper changed: her confidence. She was no longer intimidated by technology. She saw AI as a collaborator, a creative partner that worked tirelessly beside her.

By mid-2025, Mia's brand had grown into a thriving one-person media company. She was producing branded ads for other entrepreneurs, automating their social media calendars, and even offering video creation packages powered entirely by AI workflows. Her clients loved the results — polished, fast, and affordable. Many assumed she had a production team. They didn't realize her entire studio fit inside her laptop. "The secret," Mia often told them, "isn't being the best editor — it's being the fastest thinker." AI gave her that speed.

When asked what advice she'd give to new creators, Mia smiled. "Start now. Don't wait until you have a camera or studio. The tools exist. The audience exists. What's missing is your message." She believed that the new digital gold rush wasn't about who could record, but who could communicate. Her story became a beacon for thousands of creators who once thought video marketing was out of reach. Through her journey, she proved that the era of AI video creation isn't just about technology — it's about reclaiming creative freedom.

As her latest short hit two million views, Mia looked at her analytics dashboard — a screen filled with numbers, charts, and growth curves — and whispered to herself, "I didn't need a camera. I just needed courage." That's the essence of this new era. Technology is no longer the barrier — hesitation is. The tools are ready, the world is watching, and those who dare to create with AI will lead the future of storytelling

Chapter 2: From Script to Screen — How to Turn Ideas Into Viral Videos With AI

Every viral video begins with a single idea — a thought, message, or insight that captures human attention. But in the fast-moving world of digital marketing, ideas are worthless unless they're executed quickly. The average content trend on platforms like TikTok or Instagram Reels lasts less than ten days, and if you can't transform your concept into a shareable video fast, someone else will. That's why Artificial Intelligence has become the single most powerful accelerator for modern creators. With the right combination of AI tools, you can turn a raw idea into a viral, polished video — ready to publish — in less than an hour. This chapter will teach you how to do exactly that.

The process begins with **concept generation**. AI tools like ChatGPT or Claude can instantly generate hundreds of video ideas tailored to your niche, audience, and tone. For instance, if you run a fitness brand, you can prompt ChatGPT with: *"Give me 20 viral short-form video ideas about staying fit for busy parents."* Within seconds, you'll have titles, hooks, and storylines. But here's where strategy comes in: not every idea deserves execution. Focus on those that provoke emotion — surprise, inspiration, or transformation. Emotional engagement drives virality more than production quality ever will. AI can even help you analyze audience sentiment by summarizing top comments or viral trends within your niche, ensuring you create what people already want to share.

Once you've selected your idea, it's time to **script it with precision**. Most short-form videos under 60 seconds follow a proven formula: *Hook → Value → Emotion → Call to Action.* AI can generate this entire flow for you. Example prompt: *"Write a 45-second video script that starts with a shocking statistic about financial freedom, teaches one quick lesson, and ends with a motivational call to action."* The AI will produce a ready-to-use script in seconds, complete with pacing, transitions, and emotional beats. You can then refine it to match your tone or brand voice. The secret is brevity. The shorter and clearer your message, the more the algorithm will favor it. Viewers decide within 1.3 seconds whether to keep watching — so your opening line must grab attention immediately. Let AI help you test multiple hooks and select the most engaging one.

Now comes **visual generation and production**. Tools like **InVideo** and **Pictory** allow you to paste your script directly into the platform, automatically matching visuals, captions, and background music. You can choose from templates — educational, cinematic, motivational, product-based — and watch as the software builds a fully edited video in real time. For faceless creators, this is revolutionary. You can create professional content without ever appearing on camera. If you want a human presence, **Synthesia** lets you add AI avatars that look realistic and speak in your voice. You can even clone your voice or choose from hundreds of multilingual options, opening global markets instantly. What used to require filming equipment, lighting, and hours of editing can now be done from your browser in minutes.

Once your first draft video is ready, use **AI editing and enhancement tools** like **OpusClip** to refine it. Upload your video, and the AI will automatically identify the best segments, trim dead time, add dynamic captions, and even analyze emotional peaks using data from millions of viral videos. It essentially acts as a professional editor — except it never sleeps, and it learns what works best for your audience every time. You can generate multiple versions of the same video, each optimized for different platforms: one with subtitles and quick cuts for TikTok, one with widescreen and voiceover for YouTube, and another with a clean, corporate look for LinkedIn. The power lies in repurposing — AI lets you multiply one idea into an entire campaign.

The final step is **distribution and optimization**. Platforms like **Metricool**, **Buffer**, or **VidIQ** now use AI to predict the best posting times, hashtags, and thumbnail styles for your specific audience. You can automate scheduling so your videos post when engagement is highest, even while you sleep. The system will track your watch time, completion rates, and click-throughs, feeding data back into your creative loop. This continuous optimization cycle ensures that every new video performs better than the last. The more content you publish, the smarter your AI system becomes — just like a personal marketing assistant that evolves with you.

But perhaps the most important part of this entire process is **mindset**. Many creators still think AI makes their content less personal, when in reality it makes it more effective. By removing the technical workload, AI allows you to focus entirely on storytelling, emotion, and strategy. The screen may be powered by code, but the connection is still human. If you use AI as your creative amplifier rather than your replacement, you'll produce videos that not only go viral — they'll build real trust, community, and brand loyalty. The next wave of successful marketers won't be those who simply create videos; they'll be those who systemize video creation through AI and storytelling synergy.

This chapter is your launchpad. Once you learn to go from script to screen in one seamless AI-powered workflow, your production capacity becomes limitless. You'll be able to dominate your niche with consistent, engaging, and automated content. In the age of AI, consistency plus creativity equals unstoppable growth. It's time to stop worrying about perfection — and start creating faster than ever.

"One Hour to Viral"

Jordan Lee had always dreamed of becoming a motivational speaker, but between his full-time job and family, he never had the time or resources to film videos. He watched creators on TikTok grow from obscurity to millions of followers, wondering how they did it. One night, after scrolling through another wave of motivational clips, he decided to experiment with AI tools he'd heard about. "What if I could make one viral video in an hour?" he whispered to himself. That question would change his life.

He opened ChatGPT and typed: *"Write a 45-second motivational video script for people who feel stuck in life."* Within seconds, the AI responded with a script that started with a bold hook: *"You're not tired — you're uninspired."* Jordan smiled. It was perfect. He copied the text and opened **InVideo**, pasting the script into a pre-built motivational video template. The software automatically added stock clips of people working out, city skylines, and sunrise time-lapses. Then it overlaid captions in bold white text, synchronized to a deep, cinematic background track. Within minutes, the preview was complete. Jordan could hardly believe what he was seeing — it looked like something a professional agency would produce.

He decided to take it further. He cloned his voice using **ElevenLabs** and imported the narration into InVideo. The AI perfectly aligned his voice with the visuals, matching every beat with emotion. In less than 30 minutes, he had a finished video that felt powerful, authentic, and completely his own — despite never touching a camera. He uploaded it to TikTok with the caption *"You're not stuck — you're one decision away from changing everything."* Then he went to bed.

By morning, his phone was buzzing non-stop. Over 120,000 views overnight. Comments poured in: *"I needed this today." "Bro, how did you make this?" "This hit me so hard."* The algorithm had picked up his post and pushed it to motivational content feeds across the platform. By the end of the week, it had crossed 1.2 million views. Jordan was stunned — he had gone viral without filming a thing.

Encouraged, he built a daily workflow. Each morning, he'd generate three new ideas using ChatGPT, pick one, and turn it into a video using InVideo and OpusClip. In under an hour, he was producing polished videos that looked like they came from a full production team. His TikTok grew to 100,000 followers in two months. People began asking him for coaching on mindset and productivity — and he realized he had just built his dream career, accidentally. His content was doing the talking for him.

Soon, Jordan started offering online workshops on “How to Build Your Brand With AI Video.” He shared every tool, every workflow, every shortcut. His students — from small business owners to teachers — began replicating his results. Many of them had never recorded a video before, but within weeks they were producing viral content. Jordan’s mission evolved: he wasn’t just motivating people anymore; he was empowering them to share their message fearlessly. His success became proof that AI wasn’t replacing human creativity — it was amplifying it.

Months later, as he looked at his analytics dashboard showing millions of total views, he smiled and thought back to that night when he almost gave up. All it took was one question, one script, and one AI-powered video to change everything. “Anyone can go from script to screen,” he said in his next viral clip, “but only those who start today will own tomorrow.” His followers flooded the comments with fire emojis, inspired once again. Jordan had found his rhythm, his audience, and his voice — all through the power of AI.

The era of waiting for perfection was over. He was living proof that one idea, one prompt, and one hour could be enough to change your life forever.

Chapter 3: Mastering Faceless Video Marketing

The idea that you must appear on camera to succeed in video marketing is officially outdated. Welcome to the era of **faceless video marketing**, where creators, brands, and entrepreneurs build massive audiences without ever showing their faces. This movement has exploded across YouTube, TikTok, and Instagram — not out of fear or shyness, but because AI tools have made it possible to tell powerful visual stories anonymously. Whether you're an introvert, a busy professional, or simply prefer to keep your private life private, faceless video creation offers an unlimited path to influence and income. And the best part? With AI, you can produce high-quality, emotionally resonant videos that perform just as well — and often better — than traditional on-camera content.

Faceless content works because it focuses entirely on **message and emotion**, not personality or appearance. Viewers don't stay for your face; they stay for your value. In fact, faceless videos often perform better because they rely on powerful visuals, music, captions, and storytelling — all of which AI now handles with precision. Tools like **Pictory**, **InVideo**, and **OpusClip** allow you to combine stock footage, text overlays, and voiceovers to produce captivating shorts and reels in minutes. You simply paste your script, choose a tone (motivational, educational, cinematic, or calm), and let the AI assemble it. Add subtitles and trending background music, and suddenly, you have a scroll-stopping video that looks like it was made by a creative agency — without ever hitting "record."

The secret to mastering faceless videos is mastering **contextual storytelling**. Every successful video answers one of three subconscious viewer questions: *Can this help me? Can this inspire me? Can this entertain me?* When you create faceless content, your visuals must amplify the emotional message behind the script. For example, if your topic is perseverance, AI can select scenes of sunrise runs, mountains, or people pushing through challenges. If your focus is financial freedom, the AI might choose symbolic imagery like open roads, digital screens, or ocean waves. Every clip becomes a metaphor, helping your audience feel the message rather than just hear it. This is how faceless videos connect on a deep emotional level — by turning abstract ideas into visual poetry.

Once your script and visuals are aligned, the next pillar is **voice and sound design**. Voice carries emotion. You can use AI narration tools like **ElevenLabs**, **Play.ht**, or **Synthesia** to generate natural-sounding voices that match your brand tone — whether authoritative, friendly, or inspirational. You can even clone your voice for consistency without recording new audio every time. For background music, platforms like **Soundraw**, **Beatoven**, or **Epidemic Sound** can automatically generate or select tracks that fit the mood of your message. A good audio mix can instantly elevate a faceless video from average to unforgettable. Remember: viewers often feel before they think. Let AI help you trigger that emotional response.

The next level of faceless mastery is **automation and scalability**. Once you've built a repeatable system, you can batch-produce 10–20 videos per week effortlessly. Use **ChatGPT** to generate daily prompts and scripts. Let **InVideo** create your visuals. Run those through **OpusClip** to generate short versions for every platform. Schedule them with AI-powered tools like **Metricool** or **Repurpose.io**, and let your content ecosystem grow while you sleep. You're no longer just a creator — you're a media brand operating on autopilot. Consistency becomes easy when production friction disappears.

However, even faceless videos must feel **authentic**. Avoid generic stock visuals that look robotic or repetitive. Customize your imagery to fit your narrative. Add your own text overlays, subtle branding, or logo watermark. Speak directly to your audience in the script as if you were face-to-face. The more personal your storytelling feels, the more trust you'll build. People might not see your face, but they'll feel your personality through your words, tone, and rhythm. That's what creates loyalty — not visibility, but relatability.

Finally, understand that faceless video marketing is not just a shortcut; it's a strategy for long-term brand scalability. You can create multiple channels or accounts under different themes — motivational, financial, educational, or lifestyle — all powered by AI. Each can become its own income stream through ad revenue, affiliate links, or digital product sales. This is how modern creators multiply themselves — by separating their identity from their production. The system, not the individual, becomes the star.

The faceless revolution has already begun. From AI-narrated documentaries to animated explainers and faceless YouTube automation channels earning six figures a year, the landscape is full of opportunity. AI has democratized storytelling in a way that no camera ever could. It has given creators control over scale, speed, and privacy — all at once. So whether you're shy, strategic, or simply efficient, faceless video marketing is your gateway to limitless creative and financial freedom. In this new era, your face is optional — but your voice, your ideas, and your consistency are everything.

"The Invisible Creator"

For years, Daniel Kim worked behind the scenes at a marketing agency, editing videos for influencers who basked in fame while he stayed invisible. He knew every trick — how to color-correct, sync music, and create emotional hooks — but he never once considered putting his own content out there. "I'm not the type," he'd say whenever someone encouraged him to start a channel. He didn't want the pressure of being on camera or dealing with online criticism. Still, deep down, he felt frustrated. Every time he helped someone else's video go viral, a small voice whispered: *That could have been you.*

In 2024, Daniel discovered **faceless video marketing** through a Reddit thread titled "How I Built a 100K Channel Without Showing My Face." The post described using **Pictory** and **ElevenLabs** to create daily motivational videos in minutes. Curious, Daniel experimented that weekend. He opened ChatGPT and typed, *"Write a 60-second motivational video script about never giving up."* The AI produced a beautiful, cinematic monologue that sounded exactly like the kind of content he loved editing. He pasted the script into Pictory, chose "inspirational" as his tone, and watched the platform assemble clips of mountains, runners, and golden sunrises. He added a deep male AI voice and soft piano music. Within 20 minutes, his first video was ready.

He uploaded it to YouTube with no expectations. Three days later, the video had over 30,000 views. The comments flooded in: *"This hit me hard." "Exactly what I needed." "Whoever made this, thank you."* Nobody knew his name, and that anonymity felt liberating. For the first time, Daniel's message spoke louder than his identity. The invisible creator had finally found his audience.

Encouraged, he built a system. Each morning before work, he used ChatGPT to write three new motivational scripts. He ran them through Pictory and added custom captions, quotes, and background tracks. By automating the process, he was able to release one video every day for 90 days straight. His subscriber count exploded past 200,000. He began earning ad revenue and affiliate commissions linking to self-improvement courses and AI tools he used himself. His inbox filled with partnership offers, yet nobody had ever seen his face. The irony wasn't lost on him — the man who once refused to be seen was now seen by millions every week.

Daniel's content became known for its emotional intensity. People felt like his videos "spoke directly to them." Viewers would comment things like, *"I don't know who you are, but your words saved me today."* That invisible connection became his superpower. He realized that faceless content allowed him to focus entirely on storytelling — no ego, no distractions, just message. It wasn't about him; it was about impact.

Over time, Daniel launched a second faceless channel focused on entrepreneurship, then a third about relationships and mindset. Each one followed a slightly different tone but used the same AI-powered workflow. Within a year, his network generated enough income for him to quit his agency job. He created a digital course called *"Faceless Freedom: How to Build a Viral Channel Without Showing Your Face,"* which sold thousands of copies worldwide. Ironically, he never appeared in the course videos either — only his voice did, crisp and confident, backed by cinematic visuals.

When asked during a podcast interview why he never showed his face, Daniel simply said, "Because it's not about me — it's about the message. I want people to hear the voice in their head that tells them to keep going, not to see mine." That quote became viral itself, spreading across social media as screenshots and clips.

Today, Daniel's faceless videos reach over 50 million views a month. He employs a small remote team to handle scheduling and analytics, but he still writes every script himself — quietly, anonymously, powerfully. He no longer hides out of fear; he chooses invisibility as a form of creative freedom. His story proves that influence isn't defined by visibility. It's defined by the courage to share your message — with or without a camera.

Chapter 4: AI Storytelling Secrets – How to Hook, Engage, and Retain Viewers in 30 Seconds

Storytelling has always been the heartbeat of marketing, but in today's digital era, it must move at the speed of a swipe. The average viewer scrolls through hundreds of videos per day and gives you less than three seconds to earn their attention. Traditional storytelling structures no longer work – they're too slow. To thrive in this environment, you need a new formula: **AI-assisted micro-storytelling**, where artificial intelligence helps you compress emotion, value, and action into 30 unforgettable seconds. The best part is that AI can now analyze, predict, and even construct stories optimized for retention, making it easier than ever to capture attention and keep it.

The foundation of viral storytelling is **the hook**. Your first three seconds determine everything. AI tools such as ChatGPT, Jasper, or Notion AI can generate hundreds of hooks based on emotion, curiosity, and data-driven phrasing. A great prompt to start with is: *"Write 10 emotionally charged video hooks that make viewers stop scrolling on Instagram Reels about [your topic]."* The AI will produce variations using psychological triggers like surprise, relatability, and tension.

You'll notice patterns — questions, challenges, and bold statements perform best. For instance, "You've been lied to about success" or "This is why your dreams aren't working." Once you test a few, the AI can even predict engagement levels using past analytics. The science of grabbing attention is now automated.

After the hook comes **the emotional bridge** — the part where you build a quick connection. This is where AI can analyze tone and sentiment. If your hook is intense or shocking, the bridge should offer understanding or empathy. For example, if you start with "You've been wasting years doing this wrong," follow up with, "And it's not your fault — you were taught to think that way." The AI can balance tone, ensuring your message feels motivating, not judgmental. It's this emotional modulation that keeps people listening instead of scrolling away. You can even ask AI to rewrite your script in multiple emotional styles — calm, persuasive, humorous, or empathetic — and select the one that resonates most with your brand.

Next is **the payoff** — what your story teaches or reveals. AI tools like Claude or ChatGPT can structure this section for clarity and pacing. Use the "Problem-Solution-Transformation" framework: identify a problem your viewer faces, present a simple fix, and illustrate the transformation that follows. For instance: "Most people give up after failure — here's what successful people do differently." The payoff must be specific, concise, and visual. The best short-form stories end with a clear "aha moment" that triggers a share or save. You're not just informing; you're giving the viewer a feeling of instant growth. Ask your AI writer to end your script with a statement that inspires reflection or action, like, "Now imagine where you'd be if you started today."

But storytelling isn't just words — it's rhythm. **AI video editors** such as OpusClip and Descript use data from millions of viral videos to determine ideal pacing, subtitle frequency, and cut timing. They can automatically trim slow sections, sync visuals to music, and emphasize keywords with dynamic captions. The rhythm of your story is what creates flow — the invisible beat that keeps viewers watching subconsciously. Too slow and they scroll; too fast and they disconnect. AI ensures that your timing aligns with audience behavior patterns. It's storytelling guided by neuroscience.

Another secret of high-retention videos is **pattern interruption**. Humans get bored quickly, so the AI must change visual elements every 2–3 seconds — a new clip, text overlay, zoom, or sound. InVideo and Pictory can do this automatically, switching visuals and fonts in sync with your narration. Some creators go a step further and use Midjourney or DALL-E to generate unique background images or transitions that break monotony. The goal is to surprise the brain just enough to maintain focus without overwhelming it. In short, AI helps you engineer curiosity on autopilot.

Finally, end every story with a **loop or call-to-action**. A loop re-engages the viewer by referencing the beginning of your story, creating a sense of completion. A call-to-action, on the other hand, directs their energy — "Follow for more tips," "Comment your dream goal," or "Click the link to learn how." You can even use AI analytics tools like TubeBuddy or VidIQ to test which CTAs perform best with your audience. The more interactive your endings, the more the algorithm rewards your content with reach.

In the past, crafting a compelling story required instinct and trial-and-error. Now AI provides instant feedback, emotional insight, and structural templates to make storytelling both an art and a science. It turns your raw ideas into emotionally optimized narratives that convert. The future of content isn't about who tells the story louder — it's about who tells it smarter. AI gives you that advantage: the ability to speak directly to both the human heart and the machine algorithm. In this 30-second world, stories are your greatest currency — and AI is your storyteller's compass.

"Thirty Seconds to Change a Life"

Samantha Torres was a high-school teacher by day and a dreamer by night. She'd always wanted to inspire others, but her small motivational YouTube channel never seemed to grow. She poured hours into videos that barely reached a hundred views. "Maybe I'm just not interesting enough," she sighed one evening while scrolling through Instagram. That's when she noticed something — videos shorter than 30 seconds were dominating her feed. Raw, emotional, fast. A creator explained how he used AI to craft micro-stories that went viral. Intrigued, Samantha decided to try one last experiment before giving up.

She opened ChatGPT and typed, *"Write a 30-second motivational story that starts with a powerful question and ends with an inspiring quote."* The AI replied instantly: *"Have you ever felt invisible? Like your effort doesn't matter? The truth is, someone is watching — waiting for you to rise so they can believe again."* The words hit her hard. She copied the text, opened **InVideo**, and chose a "Cinematic Inspiration" template. Within minutes, AI paired her narration with visuals of sunrise, footsteps, and city lights. She uploaded her first short with trembling hands and went to bed.

The next morning, her phone was blowing up. Thousands of views. Hundreds of comments. One message read, *"I cried. I really needed this today."* Samantha sat speechless, tears welling in her eyes. For years, she had tried to be perfect – rehearsing long videos, worrying about lighting and makeup – but now, with one 30-second AI-crafted story, she had reached more people than ever before. That day, she realized that storytelling wasn't about presentation. It was about precision.

Encouraged, Samantha built a routine. Every night, she used AI to write five new micro-stories. Some began with hooks like "The day you almost quit might be the day you succeed." Others used metaphors: "A seed doesn't bloom under pressure; it blooms after patience." She let **ElevenLabs** narrate her words with a soft, confident tone, while InVideo layered matching scenes. Each morning, she posted one clip – and every single one outperformed the last. Within a month, she had 50,000 followers and daily messages from people thanking her for her "voice." Ironically, it wasn't her voice at all; it was an AI replica trained on her first recording.

Her friends couldn't believe how fast her growth came. "You cracked the algorithm," they said. But Samantha knew better. She hadn't hacked anything – she'd just learned to tell stories in a way the digital world could hear. The AI became her creative partner, helping her compress years of experience into seconds of meaning. She started teaching others her method, launching a course called *"Storytelling in 30 Seconds,"* where she shared her exact prompts, scripts, and tools.

One night, a message arrived from a viewer named David: *"I was planning to give up on my art today, but your video stopped me. I painted again for the first time in months. Thank you."* Samantha smiled, realizing her stories were doing more than entertaining — they were changing lives. Her content had become a bridge between technology and emotion, between human pain and AI precision.

Months later, Samantha stood on a stage giving a TEDx talk titled *"The Future of Storytelling: From Heart to Algorithm."* Behind her played one of her AI-generated reels — the same 30-second video that started it all. As the audience applauded, she said, "I didn't just use AI to tell stories — I used it to remind people that they still matter."

In that moment, she understood that technology doesn't steal authenticity; it amplifies it. With the right story, even half a minute can change a life — and in her case, it changed thousands.

Chapter 5: AI Video Ads That Convert – How to Sell Without Sounding Salesy

The days of hard-selling commercials are over. Audiences today don't want to be "sold to" – they want to be **inspired, informed, and emotionally moved**. The best-performing video ads on platforms like YouTube, Meta, and TikTok no longer scream "Buy now!" They tell micro-stories, build trust, and deliver value before asking for action. Artificial Intelligence has made this approach scalable and measurable. With AI, you can craft personalized video ads that feel authentic and conversational, not robotic or pushy – and you can do it faster than any traditional marketing team ever could.

The secret to creating video ads that convert lies in **psychological sequencing**: attention, emotion, solution, and credibility. AI tools can now handle every phase of this sequence automatically. For example, **ChatGPT** or **Copy.ai** can generate ad scripts that start with a strong emotional hook ("Are you tired of wasting time editing videos that never perform?"), transition into relatability ("You're not alone – most creators struggle to keep up"), and lead into a solution ("That's why AI tools like OpusClip and InVideo are changing everything"). You can even instruct the AI to tailor the tone –

friendly, authoritative, or aspirational — based on your target audience. This ensures every ad starts like a story, not a pitch.

Next, the **visual phase** brings your message to life. Tools like **Pictory** and **Synthesia** allow you to turn those AI-written scripts into stunning, emotion-driven ads in minutes. You can generate faceless versions for broad campaigns or use AI avatars and voice cloning for personalized delivery. For instance, you could have a digital spokesperson introduce your offer, switch to dynamic visuals of your product in action, and then close with a subtle call to action — all produced automatically. The goal is immersion, not intrusion. Instead of forcing a sale, you create a narrative where the product becomes the natural solution to the viewer's emotional need.

The **emotional trigger** is what drives conversions, and AI can identify and amplify it with precision. Emotion-detection algorithms in platforms like **Synthesia**, **Lumen5**, and **VidIQ** can analyze previous ads to determine which phrases, tones, or visuals generated the most engagement. They then help you craft scripts that mirror that same emotional pattern. For example, if your audience reacts strongly to transformation stories, the AI will prioritize "before and after" structures in future ads. This emotional intelligence ensures that your message always resonates with the human side of your audience, even when it's delivered through machine-generated content.

Once your ad is ready, **A/B testing** becomes your best friend. AI-powered analytics tools like **Google Performance Max**, **AdCreative.ai**, and **Meta Advantage+** can automatically test multiple versions of your video, measure click-through rates, and allocate your budget to the top performers — all without manual effort. You can test 20 variations of a 30-second video overnight and know by morning which one converts best. AI doesn't just optimize your ad spend; it evolves your storytelling strategy in real time. The era of guessing is over — now you can measure emotional response, audience retention, and conversion triggers down to the second.

The most advanced creators are now using AI to **personalize video ads at scale**. Imagine sending each viewer a version of your ad that speaks directly to them — addressing their needs, interests, or location. Tools like **Rephrase.ai** and **Hour One** make this possible. They allow you to dynamically swap names, products, or background visuals in your videos, creating personalized experiences that feel intimate. Studies show that personalized video ads can increase conversions by over 400%. AI makes personalization not just possible, but automatic.

However, the real art lies in **subtle selling**. Viewers know when they're being manipulated — and they resist it. Instead, your ads should feel like content that provides genuine value first. Teach something, reveal a secret, or share a relatable pain point. Then, position your offer as the solution that naturally fits the story. AI can help script this perfectly. For example: "Here's how I turned one long video into 10 viral shorts — without editing anything. It's all thanks to an AI tool called OpusClip." This doesn't feel like an ad; it feels like advice. Yet it sells powerfully because it builds trust.

Finally, every AI video ad should close with a **soft, actionable invitation**. Replace "Buy now" with "Learn more," "Watch the demo," or "Start free." AI-driven marketing has shown that gentle calls to action convert better because they lower resistance. Combine this with emotional storytelling, and your ads become persuasive, not pushy — magnetic, not manipulative.

AI video advertising is the perfect marriage of art and analytics. It allows you to test creativity with data, to sell ethically with empathy, and to scale your message without losing authenticity. The more you integrate these tools into your workflow, the more consistent your results will become. Remember: in this new world, conversion is no longer about chasing clicks — it's about building emotional alignment at scale. And AI is the most powerful ally you have to make that happen.

"The Ad That Didn't Feel Like an Ad"

When Olivia Chen launched her small skincare line, she had no budget for a marketing team. She tried boosting posts on Instagram, but the ads always felt stiff and corporate — and they barely converted. "People scroll right past," she muttered one night, frustrated. She wanted her brand to feel human, not like every other product screaming for attention. Then a friend mentioned AI video ads. Skeptical but curious, Olivia decided to experiment.

She opened **ChatGPT** and typed: *"Write a 30-second ad script for a natural skincare brand that sounds like a friend giving advice, not a commercial."* Within seconds, the AI produced something remarkable: *"If you're tired of harsh products that leave your skin dry, I get it. I tried everything until I found a simple, clean routine that actually works."* Olivia smiled — it sounded like something she'd say herself. She pasted the script into **InVideo**, added soft lighting visuals, gentle piano music, and used her cloned voice from **ElevenLabs** for narration. The result? A calm, authentic video that felt like a conversation, not an ad.

She posted it as a sponsored reel on Instagram. The next

morning, her inbox exploded. Orders tripled overnight, and dozens of comments read, *"This doesn't even feel like an ad!"* or *"You sound so real and relatable."* Olivia realized she'd stumbled onto something powerful: empathy-driven AI storytelling. Instead of selling, she shared — and people connected with her message.

Encouraged, she built a new workflow. Each week, she asked AI to write five scripts from different emotional angles — self-care, confidence, and simplicity. She tested them using **AdCreative.ai**, which automatically generated thumbnails, text overlays, and multiple ad variations. Then, she ran them on Meta's automated campaign manager, which used machine learning to optimize performance. Within two months, her ad costs dropped by 60%, while her revenue tripled. Her most successful ad wasn't flashy; it was a simple 20-second story of her own skin transformation, told in her AI-cloned voice over soft visuals. It felt personal because it was — even though she hadn't filmed a thing.

As her brand grew, Olivia used **Rephrase.ai** to personalize ads for repeat customers. Each video mentioned their first names and recommended complementary products. The feedback was overwhelming: "I've never had a brand talk to me like this," one customer said. People started sharing the ads, not because they were promotional, but because they were *beautiful.* Olivia's videos became tiny stories of self-love, delivered through technology.

By the end of the year, her AI-driven campaigns had reached over two million viewers. She was invited to speak at an e-commerce summit about "The Future of Empathy in AI Marketing." On stage, she shared her philosophy: "If your ad feels like an interruption, it will fail. But if it feels like a conversation, it will sell." The audience erupted in applause.

As she walked offstage, a reporter asked if she planned to return to traditional ads. Olivia laughed. "Why would I?" she said. "AI doesn't just make ads — it makes *connections.*"

Her journey became a case study in how authenticity and AI could coexist. She had proved that selling doesn't require shouting — just understanding. The ad that didn't feel like an ad had turned a small skincare startup into a global brand.

Chapter 6: Automating Video Production — How to Build a 24/7 Content Machine With AI

In the traditional world of content creation, consistency was the hardest part. You could make a great video today – but then what? Maintaining daily or weekly production required planning, scripting, filming, editing, and posting. For most creators and businesses, this process became exhausting and expensive. But AI has flipped the script entirely. Today, you can automate 80–90% of the video creation process using integrated AI systems that never sleep, never complain, and never miss a deadline. This chapter will show you how to build a 24/7 **AI-powered content machine** that continuously generates, edits, and publishes videos across multiple platforms – even while you're offline.

The core concept is **the automation pyramid**, which consists of three layers: *idea automation, production automation, and distribution automation.* Each layer builds upon the other, creating a seamless loop of content generation and growth. Let's break it down.

1. Idea Automation: Your content machine begins with consistent input – ideas. AI tools like **ChatGPT**, **Notion AI**, or **Jasper** can generate endless content prompts based on trending topics, audience interests, or your niche keywords. You can even automate this step using tools like **Google Trends**, **Exploding Topics**, or **Feedly**, which integrate with automation platforms like **Make.com** or **Zapier**. For instance, you can set a workflow where every time a new trend appears in your chosen topic (e.g., "AI video marketing" or "financial freedom"), the system automatically sends that topic to ChatGPT with a prompt like: *"Write a 60-second educational video script about this trend."* The output becomes your next video script, ready for production — no human brainstorming required.

2. Production Automation: Once the script is ready, the next step is generating the video itself. This is where tools like **InVideo**, **Pictory**, and **Synthesia** shine. You can integrate them with automation tools using APIs or webhooks so that each new script automatically triggers video creation. Imagine uploading a spreadsheet or Google Sheet with 100 video titles and seeing AI create 100 fully edited videos — captions, music, transitions, and all — within hours. With **ElevenLabs** or **Play.ht**, you can even automate voiceovers using your cloned voice. You no longer need to record or edit manually. The machine handles production from start to finish.

3. Distribution Automation: Once your videos are

generated, AI can handle posting, scheduling, and analytics. Tools like **Metricool**, **Repurpose.io**, and **Later** allow you to automatically publish content across multiple platforms — YouTube, TikTok, Instagram, LinkedIn, and Facebook — all optimized for each format. You can predefine your posting frequency, captions, hashtags, and even cross-post to different platforms with variations. Some systems use predictive analytics to determine the best posting times based on when your followers are most active. Others analyze your past performance to recommend new content types to test. What used to take a social media manager hours now happens automatically in the background.

To take it even further, advanced creators use **AI analytics and feedback loops**. Tools like **VidIQ**, **TubeBuddy**, and **Google Performance Max** provide real-time insights on what's performing best — watch time, click-through rate, and audience retention. You can connect these analytics directly to ChatGPT or Jasper to automatically generate new scripts based on your best-performing content. For example: "Rewrite my top-performing video on AI storytelling in a new style that appeals to entrepreneurs." The system learns from your success and continuously improves. You've now built an intelligent, evolving ecosystem.

This kind of automation doesn't just save time — it multiplies impact. You can produce 10 times more content without burnout, maintain omnipresence across platforms, and constantly feed the algorithms that drive discovery. The creators and businesses who master this will dominate digital attention. When your competitors are spending three days editing one video, your AI machine can publish 30.

However, automation must still be guided by **human strategy**. The machine handles production, but you provide the vision. Decide what themes matter, what emotions you want to evoke, and what brand message you want to reinforce. The goal isn't to replace your creativity — it's to free it. By automating the repetitive tasks, you create more room for innovation and storytelling.

In the new economy of attention, consistency builds trust. AI automation ensures you never disappear from your audience's feed. Your message stays active, your brand stays visible, and your sales funnel never stops flowing. Once set up, your 24/7 content machine becomes your most valuable digital asset — working tirelessly while you focus on growth, partnerships, or simply enjoying your freedom. Automation isn't about losing control; it's about gaining leverage. And with AI, you now have the ultimate creative leverage in human history.

"The Creator Who Never Stopped Posting"

Marcus Reed was a personal finance coach with a problem: he could create great videos, but not consistently. He'd film once a week, edit on weekends, and burn out trying to keep up with the algorithms. Every time he took a break, his views dropped, his engagement fell, and his sales slowed. "It's impossible to compete," he sighed. One night, after reading an article about AI video automation, he decided to build something radical – a content machine that never stopped posting.

He started small. Using **ChatGPT**, Marcus generated 30 video ideas in his niche: budgeting, credit repair, and passive income. For each topic, the AI wrote a short educational script. Then he fed those scripts into **InVideo**, where AI automatically produced videos with relevant footage, captions, and upbeat background music. To narrate them, Marcus uploaded a few samples of his voice into **ElevenLabs** and created a digital clone. Within 48 hours, he had a full month of professional videos ready to go – all without touching a camera.

Next, he connected **Make.com** to automate his workflow. Whenever ChatGPT produced a new script, the system automatically sent it to InVideo, which generated the video, and then uploaded it to a Google Drive folder. From there, **Metricool** scheduled daily uploads across YouTube Shorts,

TikTok, and Instagram Reels. Each post included AI-generated captions, hashtags, and thumbnails. It was flawless. For the first time, Marcus wasn't chasing deadlines — he was ahead of them.

As the weeks went by, his growth exploded. His follower count jumped from 20,000 to 150,000 in three months. Viewers began commenting things like, "You're everywhere!" and "How do you post so consistently?" What they didn't know was that Marcus's videos were being created and uploaded while he slept. His AI system worked 24/7, pulling new ideas from trending finance topics and turning them into daily posts. All Marcus did was review performance every Sunday, give the system a few new prompts, and let automation handle the rest.

One morning, while sipping coffee, Marcus realized something profound: he had achieved the dream of true digital freedom. His business continued growing even when he wasn't working. His automated content drove leads to his coaching programs, online courses, and affiliate partnerships — all while he spent more time with his family. "I finally work for ideas, not hours," he said proudly.

He later shared his workflow in a webinar titled *"The 24/7 Creator System."* Thousands of attendees tuned in. He showed how to connect tools like ChatGPT, InVideo, OpusClip, and

Metricool in a seamless loop. He even demonstrated how to use **VidIQ** analytics to teach ChatGPT which scripts performed best, creating a self-improving content engine. His audience was stunned. One viewer commented, *"You built an AI version of yourself."* Marcus smiled. It wasn't about replacing himself — it was about amplifying himself.

A year later, Marcus's automated ecosystem ran multiple channels in different niches — all faceless, all AI-powered. He had built an empire of influence that operated around the clock. When asked if he ever feared that automation would make his content feel impersonal, he replied, "Not at all. AI gives me the freedom to focus on creativity — not the grind."

He had become the living embodiment of the modern creator — a human powered by machines, using AI not as a crutch, but as an extension of imagination. Marcus's story became proof that in the age of automation, consistency isn't about discipline anymore — it's about design. And once you design the right system, your voice never stops working for you.

Chapter 7: Monetizing AI Video Content — From Views to Income Streams

Creating videos is powerful. But creating videos that make money — automatically — is transformational. AI video marketing isn't just about generating content; it's about building **sustainable, diversified income streams** that grow with every view, click, and share. In this chapter, we'll explore how to turn your AI-powered video creation system into a profit engine that earns 24/7 through multiple monetization channels: ad revenue, affiliate marketing, product sales, sponsorships, and digital assets.

The first and most accessible stream is **ad revenue**. Platforms like YouTube, Facebook, and TikTok reward consistent content creators with monetization programs based on views, watch time, and engagement. The key to unlocking this income is volume and consistency — two areas where AI automation shines. Once your AI workflow is producing daily or weekly videos, you'll quickly hit platform thresholds for monetization. On YouTube, you'll need 1,000 subscribers and 4,000 watch hours or 10 million Shorts views. AI allows you to reach these numbers exponentially faster by producing content nonstop. Each video becomes a digital employee — working for you around the clock, attracting views, and generating passive income long after it's posted.

Next comes **affiliate marketing**, one of the most lucrative ways to monetize faceless and educational content. Every time you mention a product, tool, or service in your videos, you can include an affiliate link in your description or bio. When viewers click and buy, you earn a commission. AI makes this incredibly efficient: it can automatically insert product mentions into your scripts, create matching visuals, and generate short CTA phrases like "Check the link in the description." You can even use ChatGPT to write SEO-optimized video descriptions with embedded affiliate keywords. The best-performing creators combine multiple affiliate partnerships across their videos, building long-term recurring income without ever selling directly.

For educators, coaches, and entrepreneurs, **digital product sales** offer even greater scalability. You can create courses, eBooks, or templates once and let AI-powered videos drive constant traffic. Tools like **Pictory** and **OpusClip** can turn your course highlights or book excerpts into short promo clips. Combine that with an automated funnel – built using **Systeme.io**, **ClickFunnels**, or **Kajabi** – and you have a perpetual motion machine for sales. Every short-form video becomes a top-of-funnel asset that leads viewers toward a paid product. You're not just entertaining; you're converting.

Another powerful stream is **brand sponsorships**. Once you build an audience in a niche — even a small one — companies will pay you to feature their tools or services. What's fascinating is that AI can help you attract sponsors faster by analyzing your audience demographics, engagement rates, and niche alignment. Tools like **Influencity** and **Aspire.io** use AI to match creators with brands based on performance data. You can even use ChatGPT to write outreach messages that feel natural and professional. Unlike traditional influencer deals that rely on appearance or personality, faceless creators now secure sponsorships purely based on content quality and audience trust — both of which AI helps optimize.

One of the most overlooked income streams is **repurposed content licensing**. With AI-generated videos, you can produce evergreen content and license it to other creators or companies for reuse. For example, a motivational AI video could be sold to personal development channels that need daily uploads. You can also distribute your content on multiple platforms — YouTube, Facebook, Instagram, Pinterest, and Rumble — multiplying your revenue sources without extra work. AI scheduling tools make this simple. Every platform pays differently, but they all reward consistency and quality — two things AI guarantees.

Finally, the most advanced monetization strategy is

automation stacking — using AI to integrate multiple income streams into one ecosystem. Picture this: an AI-generated short drives traffic to your YouTube channel, where viewers click your affiliate link for a course you created, which is hosted on an automated platform that delivers lessons and collects payments 24/7. That's income stacking — layered automation where every system feeds another. Each video becomes part of a self-sustaining business that grows whether or not you're actively managing it.

The beauty of AI monetization is scalability. You can build multiple channels or brands simultaneously, each targeting a different niche — finance, fitness, motivation, education, or AI tutorials. AI handles the content creation, optimization, and posting, while you collect the results. The days of trading time for money are over. You now trade **ideas for income**. Every idea you turn into an AI-generated video has the potential to become a long-term digital asset — earning indefinitely while you move on to the next creation.

In the new digital economy, attention is wealth. But the creators who win aren't those who chase trends — they're the ones who build systems. AI gives you that system: automated storytelling, automated reach, and automated revenue. Your job is simply to keep feeding the machine with vision, creativity, and authenticity. The rest runs itself. Monetization isn't magic — it's multiplication through automation. And once your AI content ecosystem is running, you'll experience the ultimate goal of modern entrepreneurship: income that flows while you sleep.

"The Day the Views Turned Into Dollars"

When Nia Patel uploaded her first AI-generated video, she wasn't thinking about money. She was a freelance designer looking to share tips on creativity and productivity. Her videos were short, simple, and faceless — elegant text overlays with her cloned voice and calming background music. Within two months, she had 40,000 followers and one viral video that hit 3 million views. One morning, while checking her analytics, she noticed a new notification from YouTube: *"Congratulations! Your channel is now eligible for monetization."* She stared at the screen in disbelief. "Wait... I can actually make money from this?"

She enabled ads and continued posting. A few weeks later, she received her first payment: $278. It wasn't much, but it was proof that her content could generate income on autopilot. That single realization changed everything. She decided to transform her creative hobby into a business.

Using **ChatGPT**, Nia generated 50 new video ideas around the topics of design, productivity, and freelancing. She created the videos with **Pictory** and **ElevenLabs**, scheduling them through **Metricool** to post twice a day. As her view count grew, she noticed her affiliate links – small mentions of tools like Canva and Figma in her video descriptions – started earning commissions too. $20 here, $40 there. Then $300. Within three months, she was earning more from her AI videos than from her freelance gigs. "I built a business without even trying," she laughed.

Encouraged, Nia launched her own digital product – a mini-course called *"Design Smarter, Not Harder."* She promoted it in her videos using short AI-generated ads that led viewers to her website. The conversion rate was incredible because her followers already trusted her voice. Her AI videos didn't feel like marketing – they felt like mentorship. Soon, her income tripled again.

To keep scaling, she built an automated funnel. ChatGPT wrote new scripts, InVideo created video lessons, and Kajabi handled the sales and delivery. Everything ran automatically. Even her email follow-ups were written and sent by AI. Nia had unknowingly built a digital business empire – run almost entirely by algorithms.

Six months later, she received an email from a productivity app offering $5,000 to sponsor one of her videos. "You've built one of the most trusted channels in your niche," the brand representative said. It hit her then: trust wasn't built through appearance — it was built through consistency and authenticity, both made possible by AI. She accepted the sponsorship and used AI again to produce a polished ad that blended seamlessly into her usual content. The audience loved it — and the brand partnership turned into a recurring deal.

One evening, sitting on her balcony overlooking the city, Nia opened her analytics dashboard: ad revenue, affiliate commissions, product sales, and sponsorship income. It was all flowing in real time. She smiled, realizing she hadn't made a video manually in months. Yet her system was earning thousands weekly.

Her story went viral among creators. When asked how she did it, Nia replied, "I stopped chasing followers and started building systems. AI doesn't make you rich overnight — it makes you consistent enough to succeed."

From that moment forward, Nia became an educator herself, teaching others how to monetize their AI video content through multiple income streams. Her students called her "the automation queen," but she just called herself lucky — lucky to live in a time when creativity and technology could work together to make freedom possible.

Chapter 8: AI Video Analytics – Tracking Performance, Growth, and ROI

In the age of AI-driven marketing, **data is the new creative compass**. The difference between creators who grow exponentially and those who stagnate isn't just effort – it's insight. The best creators don't guess what works; they measure it. AI video analytics turns raw data into actionable intelligence, helping you understand exactly what your audience loves, when they tune out, and why they buy. By mastering AI analytics, you'll move from simply creating videos to strategically scaling an entire brand backed by precision data and predictive growth models.

Traditional analytics once required manually checking metrics like views, likes, and comments. But today's AI tools dig much deeper – they read *behavioral intent*. Platforms like **VidIQ**, **TubeBuddy**, **Social Blade**, and **Google Analytics 4** now use machine learning to evaluate watch time patterns, keyword performance, audience demographics, and even emotional reactions within your videos. The AI learns from every frame – identifying which hooks grab attention, which scenes lose viewers, and which words drive the most engagement. In essence, your analytics dashboard becomes a living feedback loop — an AI mentor that teaches you how to tell better stories, one upload at a time.

To begin, focus on **three key categories** of data: engagement, retention, and conversion.

- **Engagement metrics** measure how your content captures attention. This includes likes, shares, comments, and watch percentage. AI analytics can automatically detect engagement spikes and attribute them to specific phrases, visuals, or emotional cues. For example, tools like **Pictory Insights** or **OpusClip AI** analyze your videos frame by frame to identify "moments of maximum engagement." These are your future hooks — the moments to replicate in future content.

- **Retention metrics** track how long people stay. AI visualizes this with heatmaps showing when viewers drop off. If most leave after 10 seconds, the algorithm suggests reordering your story flow or shortening your intro.

- **Conversion metrics** tell you what actions viewers take next — clicking links, joining your email list, or purchasing a product. AI can correlate conversions with specific storytelling styles, helping you optimize both creative and sales outcomes simultaneously.

Once you've established your baseline, AI can begin **predictive modeling** – forecasting your next viral moment. Advanced systems like **Google Performance Max**, **Predis.ai**, or **Metricool AI** use trend recognition to recommend topics, posting times, and ad budgets based on millions of data points. These systems don't just report what happened – they predict what will work next. Imagine having an intelligent co-producer whispering, "Post this tomorrow at 2 PM for maximum engagement," or "Use this hook again; it converts 40% higher." That's the advantage of predictive analytics – creative intuition guided by data science.

To take it further, integrate **AI sentiment analysis** tools. Platforms like **Munch**, **Clarabridge**, or **MonkeyLearn** can read thousands of comments in seconds and identify the emotions behind them – joy, anger, curiosity, inspiration. This gives you a psychological snapshot of your audience. If your AI detects recurring excitement around motivational stories but lower sentiment on tutorials, you'll know exactly where to shift your strategy. These insights are pure gold because they help you shape content that connects emotionally and converts logically.

Another crucial aspect is **ROI tracking** – especially for creators running ad campaigns or selling products. AI attribution tools such as **Hyros**, **Triple Whale**, and **Windsor.ai** can track every dollar spent on ads and every sale generated from video content. They show you not only *what worked* but *why it worked*. For example, they might reveal that videos with short text overlays produced 30% more conversions or that AI voiceovers performed better than live narration. With this level of clarity, scaling your content strategy becomes a matter of mathematics, not guesswork.

The most advanced creators use AI analytics to build **feedback automations**. Here's how it works: every week, your AI analytics tool exports a performance summary (best videos, best keywords, and audience insights) to ChatGPT or Jasper. The AI then generates new script ideas based on those winning patterns. You can connect this process through **Make.com** or **Zapier**, creating a closed-loop automation system where your analytics feed your creative pipeline. The result? Continuous improvement without manual effort – a self-optimizing video business that gets smarter over time.

But remember – data means nothing without interpretation. The goal isn't to drown in numbers but to **translate data into decisions**. Let AI handle the analysis while you focus on strategy. When your system says, "Videos with a question hook retain 40% more viewers," use that knowledge creatively. Experiment, adapt, and refine. Over time, your instincts and your AI will synchronize, giving you an almost intuitive ability to predict viral success before it happens.

AI video analytics transforms marketing from reactive to proactive. You stop chasing trends and start shaping them. The moment you treat data not as a report but as a conversation, you'll see patterns others miss. You'll know exactly what to create, when to post, and how to grow. That's the essence of intelligent content mastery — creativity enhanced by algorithmic insight. In the next era of marketing, the most successful creators won't just make great videos — they'll make **data-driven art** that inspires, performs, and profits endlessly.

"The Data Whisperer"

When Leo Ramirez started his YouTube channel about personal finance, he treated analytics like a chore. He'd upload videos, glance at the view count, and move on. "I'm a creator, not a mathematician," he used to say. But after months of unpredictable results — one video going viral, the next barely reaching 100 views — he realized creativity alone wasn't enough. If he wanted consistency, he needed clarity. That's when he discovered **AI video analytics**.

He began by connecting **VidIQ** and **TubeBuddy** to his YouTube channel. Within hours, the AI generated detailed insights. It told him that videos under 90 seconds performed best, that his audience watched mostly on mobile devices, and that his retention dropped sharply at the 12-second mark. Even more shocking, it identified that the phrase “financial freedom” drove twice as many clicks as any other keyword in his titles. “It’s like having a marketing scientist sitting beside me,” Leo whispered.

Encouraged, he dove deeper. Using **Pictory Insights**, he uploaded his top-performing videos to see which scenes kept viewers hooked. The AI highlighted the exact five-second clips that triggered the highest engagement – usually when he told personal stories instead of giving advice. That discovery changed everything. From then on, Leo structured every new video around storytelling first and education second. His retention skyrocketed, and his average view time doubled within weeks.

But Leo didn’t stop there. He integrated **Make.com** to automate weekly reports. Every Sunday, his analytics were automatically summarized and sent to ChatGPT, which generated three new video ideas based on what worked best. One of those AI-suggested topics – “How I Saved $100K

Without a Budget" — went viral, hitting 2.5 million views. The irony? The AI had written 80% of the script itself.

As his channel grew, Leo began monetizing through affiliate links and sponsorships. To optimize earnings, he used **Hyros** to track conversions from each video. The AI discovered that his motivational videos, while gaining more views, converted fewer leads than his "step-by-step" tutorials. So, he balanced both styles strategically — storytelling for reach, tutorials for revenue. His monthly income soon surpassed his old corporate salary.

Still, what fascinated Leo most wasn't the money — it was the feedback loop. He realized his channel had become a living organism, evolving automatically based on viewer behavior. Every click, comment, and share fed new insights back into the system, shaping the next video. "It's like the audience is co-creating my content with me," he said during a podcast interview.

A year later, Leo was invited to speak at a marketing summit. His presentation was titled *"The Data Whisperer: How to Let AI Tell You What to Create."* He explained how analytics wasn't about cold numbers — it was about listening to digital signals of emotion and curiosity. "The data doesn't replace creativity," he told the audience. "It refines it. It teaches you how to speak your audience's language fluently."

By the end of the talk, dozens of creators approached him for advice. One asked, "Aren't you worried AI will make all videos look the same?" Leo smiled. "Not if you use it right. AI tells me what my audience feels – it's my job to turn that into art."

Back home that night, he checked his dashboard. Another video had just crossed a million views. But instead of excitement, he felt calm. For the first time, he wasn't chasing luck – he was building predictability. His AI analytics didn't just show him numbers; they showed him patterns of human behavior, a rhythm he could finally understand. As he leaned back in his chair, he whispered, "Data is just another kind of story – and now I know how to read it."

Chapter 9: Scaling Your AI Video Brand — Building a Global Audience With Automation

Reaching an audience once meant fighting geography, budgets, and distribution networks. Today, Artificial Intelligence has erased all three barriers. With the right tools, a solo creator or small business can reach millions worldwide—automatically. Scaling an AI video brand isn't about producing more content; it's about multiplying impact through **automation, localization, and systems thinking**. This chapter shows how to use AI to expand beyond your initial audience, build global visibility, and grow your brand into a self-sustaining digital empire.

The first principle of scaling is **platform diversification**. Each platform favors different formats and algorithms. YouTube rewards long watch time and evergreen content. TikTok prioritizes trend velocity. Instagram focuses on visual appeal and shareability. AI can help tailor your videos for each one without extra effort. Tools like **OpusClip**, **Pictory**, and **Vidyo.ai** automatically convert one long video into multiple short-form variations—each resized, captioned, and timed to match the platform's algorithm. Instead of manually re-editing, you upload once and let AI create optimized versions for every channel. The more surfaces your content appears on, the more algorithmic pathways lead viewers back to you.

Next comes **language expansion**—one of the most underestimated scaling strategies. AI translation and dubbing tools such as **ElevenLabs**, **HeyGen**, and **Papercup** can instantly reproduce your videos in multiple languages using your cloned voice. Imagine publishing your content simultaneously in English, Spanish, Portuguese, and Hindi—all sounding natural and emotionally aligned. The global audience for AI-dubbed content is massive, especially in non-English markets that crave relatable creators. By localizing your content through AI, you don't just double your reach—you multiply it. Many creators see 200–300 percent audience growth within months simply by adding multilingual captions or voiceovers.

Third is **automation of community growth**. Scaling isn't just about reaching more people; it's about keeping them engaged. AI chatbots and CRM automations can handle thousands of messages, comments, and inquiries while maintaining a human tone. Using **Manychat**, **Chatfuel**, or **HubSpot AI**, you can build conversational workflows that reply instantly with personalized responses, links to products, or invitations to join your newsletter. This keeps engagement high while freeing you from endless manual replies. AI can also segment your audience automatically by interest or geography, ensuring every new video or offer reaches the most relevant viewers.

Fourth, implement **collaborative scaling through partnerships and influencer automation**. AI analytics can identify potential collaborators based on overlapping audiences and engagement patterns. Platforms like **Collabstr**, **Heepsy**, or **Influencity** use data to recommend ideal brand matches. You can then have ChatGPT draft personalized outreach messages that sound authentic, creating collaboration opportunities while you focus on content. Strategic cross-promotion is one of the fastest ways to grow: when your videos appear on multiple creators' feeds, algorithms interpret your content as "high relevance," giving you organic visibility far beyond your own followers.

The fifth strategy is **funnel integration**—connecting your growing audience to monetization. Every viral video should have a path that leads viewers toward deeper engagement: a free download, newsletter, product page, or course. AI tools such as **Systeme.io** and **ConvertKit** can automate these funnels end-to-end, tracking every click and behavior. The result is an expanding ecosystem where your AI videos drive traffic, your funnel nurtures relationships, and your automations close sales—all synchronized around the clock.

As your audience scales, **data-driven personalization** becomes essential. Global growth doesn't mean generic content; it means customized storytelling at scale. AI can analyze regional trends, cultural preferences, and seasonal shifts, then recommend localized variations of your top-performing videos. A motivational clip that resonates in the U.S. might need a different tone or imagery in Japan or Brazil. With **ChatGPT Advanced Data Analysis** and **Google Trends**, you can instruct AI to rewrite captions, adjust metaphors, or even change background music to align with local emotion and behavior patterns. Personalization becomes effortless—and infinitely scalable.

Finally, true brand scaling comes from **building systems, not just videos**. Document your AI workflows in a digital "brand playbook": how you generate ideas, edit, automate, publish, and measure. Once standardized, you can delegate or outsource without losing quality. You're not just growing a channel—you're building a media company powered by AI. This allows you to launch new verticals under your brand (finance, motivation, lifestyle, tech) while maintaining consistent tone and production speed. Every system you build multiplies your creative output without multiplying your workload.

AI has made global brand growth a mechanical process that still feels deeply personal. The creators of the future won't compete by working harder—they'll compete by automating smarter. By combining multilingual expansion, audience automation, and systemized storytelling, your AI video brand becomes unstoppable: everywhere at once, perfectly optimized, and always evolving. The moment you realize your videos are gaining followers while you sleep in different time zones, you'll know you've achieved true scale—the kind powered not by hustle, but by intelligent design.

"Everywhere at Once"

When Lina Müller started her YouTube channel from her apartment in Berlin, her dream was simple: to teach small business owners how to use AI tools for marketing. Her first videos, narrated in English using InVideo and her cloned voice, gained modest traction—maybe a few thousand views each. She was grateful, but she couldn't shake the feeling that she was missing something. One night, while reading her analytics, she noticed that nearly 30 percent of her audience was coming from Brazil and India. "They like the content," she thought, "but most probably don't understand every word." That realization sparked an idea that would change everything.

The next morning, she uploaded one of her videos into **ElevenLabs** and translated it into Portuguese and Hindi. Hearing her own voice speaking fluent Portuguese felt surreal. She created subtitled versions in both languages and scheduled them using **Metricool**. Within two weeks, her Portuguese video outperformed the English original by five times. Comments poured in: *"Finally, someone teaching AI in my language!"* Her subscriber count jumped overnight. Lina realized she had just unlocked the world.

Excited, she systemized the process. Each week, she produced three English videos, translated them into five languages, and let AI automate posting across YouTube, Instagram, TikTok, and Facebook. She connected everything through **Make.com**, so every video published itself, every comment received an automated thank-you message, and every new follower was invited to her newsletter with AI-written emails. "I don't just have an audience anymore," she laughed. "I have a network." Her analytics dashboard looked like an airline map—dots lighting up from every continent.

Soon brands began to notice. A Singapore-based software company offered her a sponsorship deal to feature their product in her tutorials. Then a Spanish tech school invited her to host a workshop—remotely, of course. Her multilingual reach made her the perfect partner for international campaigns. She no longer had to pitch; opportunities came to her inbox daily.

To keep up, Lina documented her entire system in Notion: prompts for video ideas, translation workflows, AI voice settings, and posting schedules. She hired a small virtual team to help with analytics while AI handled 90 percent of production. Within six months, her content was published in eight languages and viewed by over 10 million people. Her once-tiny Berlin studio had evolved into a global AI-powered media brand.

Yet the moment that meant the most came unexpectedly. She received an email from a student in Kenya who wrote, *"Your Hindi-dubbed video helped my small business triple its income. Thank you for making it accessible."* Lina paused, tears welling up. The message reminded her why she started—to empower entrepreneurs everywhere, not just in her own city.

When journalists later asked her secret to success, she said, "I stopped thinking local and started thinking algorithmic." She explained that scaling wasn't about working harder but creating systems that let creativity travel without her. "AI made me multilingual, multi-platform, and multi-dimensional," she said with a smile.

Today, Lina's channel generates income from ad revenue, brand partnerships, and course sales across continents. Her videos play in cafés in São Paulo, classrooms in Manila, and coworking spaces in Lagos—all while she sleeps. She's no longer just a creator; she's a global educator powered by AI. And when people tell her, "You're everywhere," she simply replies, "No—I just built systems that never sleep."

That's the magic of scaling with AI: you don't chase the world. You build the engine, and the world finds you.

Chapter 10: The Future of AI Video Marketing — Evolving With the Next Wave of Innovation

The evolution of AI video marketing is only just beginning. What we've witnessed so far—automated editing, faceless video creation, AI voiceovers, predictive analytics—is merely the first phase of a much larger transformation. The next wave will redefine how creators, businesses, and audiences interact. We're entering a world where AI doesn't just assist your creativity—it becomes your co-creator, strategist, and distribution partner. Understanding this evolution is the key to staying ahead, adapting early, and turning technological shifts into long-term advantage.

The future of AI video marketing revolves around **hyper-personalization**. Current AI tools already tailor ads and captions based on audience demographics, but soon, videos themselves will dynamically adapt to each viewer. Imagine uploading one video and having the AI automatically adjust tone, visuals, and even the narrator's emotion based on who's watching. For a young entrepreneur, the video might use fast-paced music and bold visuals; for a retiree, the same message could be slower, calmer, and more reflective. This is not speculation—it's the direction models like **Runway**

Gen-3, **Synthesia 2.0**, and **Sora** are taking, combining video rendering, real-time audience data, and emotional analytics to create content that literally *changes itself* to fit the viewer. The result will be a new kind of marketing: storytelling so adaptive it feels personal to everyone who sees it.

Another major frontier is **AI-human co-production**. Soon, creators will build entire video campaigns in natural language, simply describing their goals. You'll say, "Create three 45-second videos that compare AI tools for small businesses, one motivational, one educational, one humorous." The AI will generate, edit, voice, and even test them—presenting data-driven recommendations for which version to publish first. Tools like **OpenAI's Sora**, **Pika Labs**, and **Runway** already point toward this reality, where the line between ideation and execution disappears. This means anyone with creativity will have cinematic power. You'll no longer need a team—just your imagination and a clear direction.

The third evolution will come from **interactive video intelligence**. Videos will no longer be one-way broadcasts; they'll respond. Picture a viewer watching your AI-generated product video and being able to ask questions mid-video—"Does this work in my country?" "What's the price?"—and the AI presenter answers instantly. This fusion of video and conversational AI is being pioneered by companies like **HeyGen Live** and **Synthesia Chat Avatars**, blending marketing and customer support into a single interactive experience. Instead of pushing messages outward, creators will engage in two-way, personalized dialogues with their audiences—at scale.

Then comes **multimodal integration**, the ability for AI to combine text, voice, video, and emotion recognition seamlessly. Imagine an ecosystem where AI reads your facial expression through a webcam and adjusts the ad's tone or music in real time to match your reaction. If you smile, it lightens; if you seem skeptical, it explains more clearly. This fusion of empathy and automation will mark a massive shift in digital marketing—from guessing audience mood to *reading* it. Brands and creators who embrace emotional intelligence in their videos will rise above the noise by forging genuine connection in a world oversaturated with content.

Equally transformative is **the decentralization of video platforms**. As blockchain and AI merge, creators will soon host and monetize their videos directly through decentralized networks, eliminating intermediaries like YouTube. Smart contracts will automatically pay royalties every time someone watches or shares your content. AI will verify authenticity, manage copyright, and optimize monetization—ensuring transparency and fairness. This will create a global creator economy powered by automation, where every view translates into direct income, instantly and securely.

Finally, the future of AI video marketing will belong to those who integrate **ethics, authenticity, and creativity**. As AI becomes more powerful, the temptation to mass-produce content without meaning will grow. But audiences will always crave truth, even in a synthetic world. The creators who win will be those who combine the speed of AI with the sincerity of human storytelling. They'll use technology not to replace emotion, but to amplify it. They'll understand that the soul of every great video—no matter how advanced the algorithm—still lies in its ability to make someone *feel something real.*

The future won't favor those who resist AI—it will favor those who learn to dance with it. Your role as a creator is evolving from operator to conductor, from editor to visionary. You don't need to know every tool that will emerge; you just need to cultivate curiosity, adaptability, and purpose. The next era will reward those who ask better questions, think bigger, and move faster.

AI is not taking over creativity. It's expanding it. It's giving voice to those who were silent, tools to those who were limited, and reach to those who once had none. The marketers, educators, and dreamers who harness this power with integrity will define the digital landscape for decades to come. The revolution has already started—and the next chapter belongs to you.

"The Last Edit"

It was late at night when Amira sat in her studio, staring at her computer screen. She'd been a content creator for over a decade, watching the world of video transform—first from cameras to smartphones, then from human editors to AI tools. But tonight was different. On her screen glowed a new software interface: **Sora AI**, capable of generating entire cinematic videos from simple text prompts. She took a deep breath and whispered, "Create a short film about the future of creativity."

In less than five minutes, it was done. The AI had generated breathtaking visuals—cities floating in clouds, children painting with light, machines and humans collaborating in harmony. Amira watched, stunned. The film looked like it came from a Hollywood studio, but it had been born entirely from her imagination and one line of text. For the first time in her career, she felt both awe and uncertainty. "If AI can do all this," she wondered, "what's left for me to do?"

She decided to experiment. She uploaded the AI-generated video to her YouTube channel, added a short introduction explaining that it had been made without cameras, actors, or editing software—just creativity and AI. The video went viral overnight. Comments poured in: *"This gives me hope for the future." "It feels alive." "How did you do this?"* But among them, one stood out: *"You didn't make this. The AI did."* That comment hit her hard. Was it true?

For days, she pondered what creativity meant in this new world. Then she realized something: the AI hadn't chosen the idea. It hadn't felt the emotion behind it. It hadn't written the words that guided the visuals. It was her story—AI had simply translated it faster and more beautifully than she ever could. The tool didn't replace her; it elevated her. That insight reignited her fire.

Amira began a new project—*The Human Algorithm*—a video series exploring the intersection of emotion and automation. Every episode was co-created with AI, blending data-driven precision with raw human storytelling. She used analytics to guide the topics, AI tools like **Runway** and **Synthesia** to animate ideas, and her own narration to bring warmth and soul. The series became a global sensation, translated automatically into ten languages and viewed by millions.

People weren't watching because it was AI-made—they were watching because it made them *feel human again.*

Months later, standing on stage at a technology summit, Amira spoke to an audience of innovators, creators, and dreamers. Behind her, a massive screen displayed the words: *"AI doesn't create meaning. You do."* She explained how every great video—no matter how advanced its production—still needed a spark of humanity to connect. "The tools will change," she said, "but the mission remains the same: to make people feel, think, and act."

When her talk ended, the crowd rose in applause. As the lights dimmed, she opened her laptop backstage and looked at her AI dashboard—her 24/7 creative partner. She smiled and whispered, "Let's make something beautiful." The machine responded instantly, loading a new prompt: *"What story shall we tell next?"*

She typed: *"A story about the endless possibilities of human imagination."*

The AI began to generate new scenes, colors swirling across the screen like living art. For the first time, Amira felt at peace. She wasn't losing her place in the creative world—she was expanding it. The last edit was no longer hers alone; it was shared between her and the intelligence she helped shape.

And in that perfect balance between technology and emotion, between logic and soul, the future of AI video marketing was born—not as a replacement for creators, but as their greatest ally.

Epilogue

The Age of Limitless Creation

The world has changed. The barriers that once separated professionals from beginners, marketers from dreamers, and storytellers from audiences have dissolved. We are living in an age where a single idea, powered by Artificial Intelligence, can travel the world in seconds. You don't need a studio. You don't need a team. You don't even need to appear on camera. What you need is **clarity, creativity, and courage**—the courage to start, to adapt, and to embrace a new way of creating. This book has shown you that the future of video marketing doesn't belong to the biggest or the loudest—it belongs to those who know how to use AI with purpose.

In the beginning, video creation was slow and technical. You needed cameras, lighting, editing software, and endless hours of work. Then AI arrived and rewrote the rules. It turned the impossible into the instant. It gave every creator superpowers—the ability to write scripts in minutes, produce cinematic videos without filming, analyze engagement in real time, and automate distribution across every platform. What once required a team of specialists now takes one person and one laptop. The bottleneck is no longer technology—it's imagination. And imagination, when paired with AI, becomes limitless.

The great paradox of this era is that the more artificial intelligence evolves, the more **human authenticity matters**. Audiences crave connection more than perfection. They don't care if your video was generated by algorithms—they care whether it makes them feel seen, inspired, or understood. The best AI creators are not those who hide behind automation but those who use it to express their ideas with greater depth, empathy, and frequency. The tools handle the repetition. You handle the resonance. That balance is the foundation of the new creative economy.

If you look closely, you'll see that every major shift in media has always followed the same pattern: technology democratizes opportunity, and those who adapt early rise the fastest. The printing press amplified writers. Radio amplified voices. Television amplified personalities. The internet amplified communities. Now, AI amplifies *creators*. It multiplies what you do best and eliminates what slows you down. But the responsibility that comes with this power is profound. You are no longer just a participant in the digital world—you are a **builder of it**. Every AI-generated video you release shapes the attention, emotions, and beliefs of those who watch. Use that influence wisely.

Think about where you were when you first started reading this book. Maybe you were curious about AI tools. Maybe you were overwhelmed by how fast technology was moving. Or maybe you were looking for a way to grow your business, build your brand, or share your story. Now you know the truth: AI is not a threat to your creativity—it's a mirror that reflects it faster and farther than ever before. You don't need permission to begin. You already have everything you need to create content that informs, inspires, and transforms lives.

The future of AI video marketing will not be defined by automation alone. It will be defined by *meaningful automation*—systems that allow you to scale your message without losing authenticity. You've learned how to use AI to write, edit, translate, analyze, and monetize videos, but the most important lesson is this: every tool is only as powerful as the purpose behind it. Use these tools not just to make noise, but to make impact. Not just to grow followers, but to grow influence. Not just to earn income, but to earn trust. In a world flooded with AI content, sincerity will be your greatest differentiator.

What happens next depends on you. You can take the frameworks you've learned and build a faceless channel that earns while you sleep. You can launch your own AI-powered agency helping others automate their content. You can translate your videos into ten languages and teach globally. You can analyze your data with machine precision and predict your next viral success. The opportunities are infinite because the barriers are gone. The question isn't *can you do it*—it's *will you decide to?*

Remember this: technology is only revolutionary when it's personal. The real magic of AI is not that it can create videos—it's that it allows you to create freedom. Freedom from time constraints, from fear of failure, from technical limitations, from creative burnout. Freedom to focus on your vision, your message, and your mission. You are entering a new era of entrepreneurship where creativity and automation coexist beautifully. The winners won't be those who resist the machine—they'll be those who **partner with it** to create something that feels both infinite and deeply human.

In the years ahead, the digital world will evolve faster than ever. New tools will rise, algorithms will shift, and technologies we can't yet imagine will emerge. But one truth will remain constant: the need for real connection. As long as you lead with authenticity and purpose, AI will serve you—not the other way around. You don't have to compete with the algorithm. You just have to *collaborate with it*. When you do, you'll discover the same realization that all great creators eventually reach—that creativity was never about the medium, but about the message.

So, as you close this book, I want you to imagine the possibilities waiting for you. Picture your first AI-generated video reaching thousands, then millions. Imagine strangers leaving comments about how your message changed their perspective, inspired their day, or helped their business. Imagine waking up one morning to see your content viewed across continents and languages you don't even speak. That's the future of video marketing—and it's already here.

This is your moment to rise. Not tomorrow. Not when you have more experience. Today. Use what you've learned, start where you are, and let AI amplify what makes you unique. Because in the end, the greatest innovation isn't artificial intelligence—it's the human being wise enough to use it well. You are that creator. You are that visionary. And your time to build, inspire, and lead has just begun.

www.ingramcontent.com/pod-product-compliance
Lightning Source LLC
LaVergne TN
LVHW080531210926
848481LV00021B/2430